DRIFTING WITH MY DEMONS

Iramukatirma

ISBN 979-8-89906-322-0

Dedication

Dear Akrish and Amrish,

You are the reason I continue to drift through the shadows, seeking meaning in chaos and turning pain into purpose. In your laughter, I find faith; in your curiosity, I see the spark of stories yet to be written. No rejection, no closed door, no institution—can confine the boundless potential that lives within you.

Education should illuminate, not exclude. It should awaken, not restrict. Yet, in a world where some claim to inspire but instead stifle, you will learn that true wisdom is found beyond their gates, in the resilience you cultivate and the truths you dare to seek. *Exspiro*—the opposite of inspiration—is what they offer when they fail to see your light. But you, our children, are the breath of a new world. A world where the future is not chosen, but created.

This book is also dedicated to all the guardians, *wayshowers* and trailblazers who choose to rewrite their stories, so our children, will never have to.

Last but not least, to the generations before us, who walked a very different path, doing the best they could with the little they had, one can only hope to do you proud, as I am sure our desires were once your desires, mostly left unfulfilled. To my dear parents, thank you for providing me the safe space I needed, even when I had nothing to give in return. We may not always have been on the same page, but we are here on this page, and I am forever indebted, humbled by the love you have shown me in the face of all the darkness.

This book, these songs, are not perfect, but this moment is, and this perfect moment could not have existed without you, dear *Ama and Acha.*

A special mention to my dear uncle, Paul Millot, thank you for shining your light as I searched for my way in the dark.

Yours with love,

Iramukatirma

Contents

Oath of the Drifter

"Breathe. Be. Unchained. I break free.
Fear is but a guide.
Pain the doorway to light.
In doom we walk the path of shadow
Where time is but another window.
I stand unshaken in the storm.
I rise beyond.
I am reborn."

Pain

Pain
You never really left me
Pain
The only one that stayed
Freefalling, into a space
Between Heaven and Hell
Are we sinners, Are we sane
Are we sinners are we saints
We're no one, We're nothing
We're all just special
Pain come home
This is your
Homecoming
Pain
You never really left me
Pain
The only one that stayed

PAIN: *The Lyrics*

PAIN: *The Chapter*

Pain was the ground zero on my path of exploration. As I walked into a new chapter in my own life, I discovered how pain, was almost an illusion that could be morphed into anything you choose as part of this human experience. And here I was, ready to rewrite my story. This song is not about the romanticization of pain or minimizing its effects, it simply is a state of acceptance. Much like saying "hello pain, how can I help you?".

And so I sank into this act of creation, writing music, pouring my heart into sound – I had never been able to take formal music lessons long enough to understand or read the notes, but am so thankful to those who patiently taught me everything I know, and drawing inspiration from the universe, I began to realize none of this was really mine, that I was simply an instrument. Every time I fell, the Universe caught me in its embrace and seemed to give me everything I needed.

Music turned into my therapy, my alchemy. It was then that I decided that creation is the ultimate act of defiance against suffering. False programming causes us to be victims, but what if we could crash the system?

Can one turn pain into art, and our demons into pets? I had to find out.

Collecting all my "darkness", I directed it toward this tangible burning desire to complete the experiment. It was my beginning of the end of an era of cluelessness, at the very least.

Pain come home, this is your Homecoming: External circumstances cannot determine my self-worth

Now, when "pain" visited me, I no longer pushed it away, and gone was the fear or anxiety – it no longer had the power to activate my limbic system or my fight or flight response, with discernment of course, as the pain response in fact, has an underlying protective function.

I now partnered with my pain, knowing it has come to teach me, to show me where I still needed to grow. And every time, without fail, it seemed to bring with it the seeds of creation.

I planted them, nurtured them, and then waited for the bloom.

During my "winter season", one of the coldest I had experienced, I faced some backlash from circles I thought were my world. Perhaps this project was an unconventional thing to venture to do, with no real background or credentials in the field, even laughable. Although I still have love for the people I had to leave behind, I drew the curtains as that part of the play was over. It was now time to say thank you, with love.

I stopped explaining what I was doing and started just doing – and so the more I was judged, the more love I poured into myself, slowly conquering my demons one by one.

Just like an ancient tree, when the Universe sends in the wind to shake our leaves, we can choose to grow our roots of unconditional love a little deeper into the ground, to become the most unbreakable version of self, standing the tests of every season.

One song then turned into a mini album, and this book, is just another human testimony, proof that life is full of many possible realities, and all we really have to do, is pick one.

Through music, I found meaning in this simulation we call "life". Meaning beyond what others had decided for me – even if the universe was "pranking" me in the process and spring was nowhere in sight.

I am not my pain.

I no longer wanted to be defined or confined by my pain. What if, creating through my pain, was the universe delighting in its own existence?

This shift in awareness grew each day. Every time I hit another wall, I paused to remember: I am not the one suffering. I am the watcher, and my pain simply a portal. This realization was both liberating and grounding. It allowed me to face pain with grace, knowing that while the vessel may crumble, the essence remains eternal.

Pain and joy, creation and destruction, sinner and saint –I am learning that these opposites are not mutually exclusive but seem to be interconnected. To live is to experience both the "*yin and yang*".

Saint and Sinner: The sinner is not damned and the saint is not perfect. Both are aspects of the same being. To sin is to be human, flawed and stumbling through life. To be a saint is to rise and to strive for meaning. Yet neither label captures the whole of what we are.

Heaven and Hell: These are viewed as internal landscapes instead of external realms. In the context of this song, they exist within us, as parts of our experience. Pain, grief, and despair can feel like hell, but they also hold the potential for profound growth and awakening, which can feel like heaven.

The recognition that **"we are no one, we are nothing"** dissolves the need to cling to the binary of saint or sinner. Our ego-driven definitions seem to be illusions, and in the face of the vast universe, labels feel insignificant. To be "nothing" is simply to let go of the burden of self-judgement. Within this "nothingness", lies the place of creation closest to Source, of limitless potential.

"We're all just special"

This "specialness" is not quite about the ego. We are special because we are an integral part of the cosmic whole, living out in the space between heaven and hell, as saint and sinner, in creation and destruction. We are all special, together, taking part in each other's plays as we go along, even hurting each other in roles we take on. Through hurt we can learn to forgive, we learn compassion, we learn to overcome and outperform our past versions.

Rain

I love you
But I hate
That I love you
Like Rain, I cry
You said, you wouldn't leave
But then you did
How much is that doggy in the window
Do you see me in the window, in the window
I seek no answers, we don't need no answers
I choose love
I love you, love me, love you
I love me first
Love hurts, let it rain
We need a storm to see the rainbow
We need the rain, to heal the pain
Let it rain (Cry)
Rain heal
Let the Rain heal the pain
Heal

RAIN: *The Lyrics*

RAIN: *The Chapter*

It is worth noting that actual rain, has in fact been an element in the making of this passion project, almost like a supernatural force, while finding the right melodies and lyrics, it would indeed start to rain, maybe just incidentally but then also naturally since ours is a tropical country.

Rain, the song, written right after Pain, is comparatively "light-hearted", Rain marked the beginning of the end of Pain as I knew it.

"I Love You, but I Hate that I Love you"

This was part of my process of understanding that love is a force beyond human will, and sometimes one's mind will not listen to one, wrestling with itself in a paradox of existence – where the highest bliss and deepest suffering are bound together, rather akwardly.

Rain as a metaphor for tears and purification, just as earth thirsts for water, represents our spirit's thirst for transformation. Crying doesn't need to be seen as a weakness but a means for alchemy – dissolving the past to make way for renewal.

The heart at times, seeks permanence in an impermanent world, and betrayal, whether by a lover or friend, is part of the soul's journey in breaking the illusion of control, and releasing attachment to embrace true wisdom, and for me, singledom. I needed to become the friend I never had, and the love of my life.

"How much is that doggy in the window"

The commodification of companionship, as an object to be owned, makes one question how love can be so transactional, yet enlightenment does not really come from grasping for explanations, but from surrendering, not in defeat, but in faith.

The shift from external love to self-love (not to be mistaken for narcissistic tendencies) seems more productive.

This storm is not a curse, but a necessity. I stopped asking why, and looked for the path closest to my heart so I could experience dancing in the rain. Although the journey seems never-ending and we are constantly looking for the shortest routes, I realized we could bend time by living in the moment. I found my therapy in music, and just like how a day can feel like a year when we count the minutes waiting for it to end, it can be over in what seems like a second, when we stop watching the deceptive clock. I am just here as another example of what is possible, like many before me, sharing my experience, as I experience it.

For Sayangku (My Beloved)

FOR SAYANGKU
(my beloved): *The Lyrics*

Under the night sky

We bade you goodbye

We couldn't save you

500 grams of heart

To never feel again

10,000 types of feelings

And all I have is pain

Now you're another star

Shining upon us

Beautiful child

I hope you're smiling

On the other side

And it feels so cold

Can't bring you back

Taken away

Never thought I'd see you that day

Never thought I'd see you that way

If only.

Is all I've got

Now that you're no longer here

FOR SAYANGKU: *The Chapter*

This is a funeral hymn, releasing the agony of witnessing a soul depart too soon.

That night I could not prevent the inevitable, a night my journey as a healer took its most painful turn causing me to leave the hospital setting for 3 years. It may be my shortest chapter here, but it was also my toughest.

For Sayangku describes the anguish in understanding the inescapable reality of mortality, how sometimes death wins, even when we least expect it.

Dissecting the vessel left behind was a cruel test as I struggled to accept, that an innocent child would be taken so soon.

"If only" is the reminder of guilt that lingers after every loss, and of alternative realities the mind yearns for, yet not every longing can be fulfilled.

Though this little one is no longer here, he lives on in the stars and in the melody of this song, as his soul remains untouched, I believe smiling beyond. I have since reversed my perception of death as an "ending".

Despite the tragedy of his departure, I believe the beautiful child is greeted with warmth and light, death as a metamorphosis, for while the physical body may have succumbed, his essence has not vanished. He is now a celestial being, no longer confined by suffering. And he will live on eternally. In this knowledge, however faint, however distant, there is a fragile kind of peace, made of stardust.

Death and suffering of children being one of humanity's greatest dilemmas, I struggled to find any justification, but I believe they are little Earth Angels. We can only honor them, remember their stories and learn true compassion through their adversity, while showing kindness and love. And maybe just maybe, one day, humanity will finally ascend together so our little children no longer have to be sacrificed.

Shadow

Lost in a forest

Of blue roses, red violets

And white lies

Trapped in my shadow

Lost in a forest

Feeling hollow

Falling in a hole

Buried alive, in decay I lay

Playing on repeat

Can't feel my heartbeat

Voiceless words in my head

Singing catch us if you can

I eat my pain for dinner

Drink the rain for water

Sleeping with my shadow

Tricking me with monsters on the wall

Talking to God, dear God

The loop, is trippy

I'm tripping on this trip

Changed her name to save her game

Sold some gold and bought her freedom

SHADOW: *The Lyrics*

Cremated soulmates

Bonnie bans Clyde

I was a passenger in a ghost car

Trying to make some sense but everything's in dollars

Have cake be fake

Everyone wants a piece now pay the price

Watch her rise

Now I'm jumping seats I'm making my own beats

Drifting with my demons

Tried to die but then I found my wings

Now I ride to fly

Lost in a forest trapped in my shadow

Now I dance in the forest

Now I'm friends with my shadow

You say you love me

But when it gets dark

Are you scared of my shadow

Sh sh sh Shadow

SHADOW: *The Chapter*

Shadow, was born in an otherworldly realm with distorted lenses. As I wandered through the underworld of the self, confronting all the darkest recesses of my soul, I found myself isolated, scared not of the shadows, but of what lies in the light.

The Shadow is not just the absence of light, but the unacknowledged self, the darkness we carry but refuse to face. Ingrained deep within our DNA, in voices of ancestors long gone, our souls long to break free from all the chains that held us back, and this calling grew so loud I had no choice but to answer.

To be trapped in one's shadow is to be caught in one's own fears, regrets, and suppressed truths.

The hollowness is the emptiness that comes from rejecting the self, from disowning what is meant to be integrated.

Decay, is simply the process of breaking down what no longer serves, shedding what is false to reveal what is real.

When the heartbeat is silent, there is almost a detachment from feeling, and voiceless words come from memories that haunt but do not heal, a taunt from our shadow self to chase ghosts and illusions that can never be caught because they were never really there.

Suffering becomes a form of sustenance if we allow the self to consume it. This was my process of trying to observe the pain instead and to not be deceived by the "monsters on the wall" that are simply projections of the mind, warped versions of self that may not be real, even if they appear real.

God appears in the moment of crisis, yet the presence of the divine does not always bring immediate relief and sometimes the loop continues, unconsciously creating vicious cycles, as spiritual awakening is more of an unraveling than a revelation.

I find it requires the shifting of perspective, and more often than not, it requires more than one single process, just like a chemical experiment would in a science laboratory.

As humans we often use "fate" in romanticizing connections that were "meant to last forever" yet perhaps one could challenge this notion and rewrite the classic tragedy in an exercise of free will.

In a world that only speaks in currency, the search for meaning, lies in the knowing that worth is measured in wisdom. And wisdom is true wealth.

When demons are no longer enemies, they simply become companions on the journey so our wings once hidden in the darkness, can finally emerge. When we remember our "true self" in its highest potential, finally escaping the loops that once trapped us, we alter old blueprints and build new circuits. This is when I started "drifting with my demons".

The self can integrate with its darkness, embracing it as part of a whole. It is a true measure of devotion to love oneself in its totality, replacing fear with a sense of adventure, very much like Alice's journey through Wonderland.

Life too, often reflects Wonderland's shifting, nonsensical nature, where logic is fluid, time is meaningless and nothing is as it seems, and it is easy to lose the sense of self as we descend deeper into this strange, disorienting world, meeting tricksters that force one to question reality and identity.

Yet we can escape the "loop" by simply refusing to play the roles we assign ourselves. And as Alice's journey ends when she realizes that Wonderland is a construct, a dreamscape born from her own subconscious, she does not defeat Wonderland, but wakes from it.

Similarly, perhaps our purpose is not to destroy the shadow, but to befriend it.

Mirror

Mirror Mirror on the wall

Who is the baddest of us all

Do you hate me, you don't like me? Oh no…

Well I am the you in me you see

I am the mirror

And I still love you

Outdo, Outsmart, Outshine, Outlast

I believe in me

You tried to hurt me

Well I am the Monsterpiece

You created

Wearing hearts on my fingers

Heart on my sleeve

Even if I do a hundred takes

Just to prove my first was best

Mirror mirror on the wall

Who is the baddest of us all

You are the baddest of 'em all

Unbreakable, Unshakeable, Unbeatable, Undefinable

Said the mirror

They tried to take their tokens

MIRROR:
The Lyrics

Leave me broken

Take my home, take my house

Can't take my honour

Take my candy, take my car

Can't take my courage

I'm just the Mirror, I am the Mirror

MIRROR: *The Chapter*

Mirror was written in the face of betrayal, simply as an attempt to reclaim the narrative by redirecting the story. Dispelling outdated labels, turning "bad" into "baddest" was an idea of taking what was meant to break us, and using it as the foundation for positive change.

In the original fairytale Snow White, the mirror seemed to reflect the "evil queen's" inner obsession, ego, envy and insecurities while Snow White embodies kindness, innocence, humility and a loving spirit. "The mirror", being objective, recognizes virtue over vanity. Betrayal, like the mirror, reflects not just what others have done to us, but how we respond to it.

Betrayal, in its core, can feel like destruction – tearing apart trust, relationships, and even parts of our identity. The betrayal in Mirror however, becomes the tool for one to grow into the "baddest," someone who can't be defined or diminished by the actions of others.

Sometimes this process is one of trial and error, and may require many different takes, but what matters, as they say, is the journey.

External losses – whether material or emotional, cannot touch the essence of who we are, if one is determined enough in transforming the experience into triumph. It was my chance to thrive forward boldly and unapologetically, not just to survive the moment.

The "mirror" of our experiences can either shatter us or show us our true strength. It does not just reflect struggle, it reflects victories too. It is a choice to be made, and one can choose to redefine, realign and redesign, all while reflecting onto others the love that radiates within.

Resilience, to "outlast" is to acknowledge that belief in oneself arises not from the absence of struggle but the willingness to endure it. And instead of succumbing, we can transform, combining both the monstrous and the artistic, through the duality in this existence, on a journey to becoming a master alchemist. I am but a student and life my greatest teacher.

Rise

We are one

You and me, we are one

All is love

We're under the same sky

Under the same sun

Under the same moon

Under the same stars

Like drops of water

Looking for the ocean

Drops of water looking for the sea

Drops of water

Rise

Break the system

We are one, you and me, we are one

This is a war against war

Rise

We are one

RISE: *The Lyrics*

RISE: *The Chapter*

Rise is an anthem of unity and awakening, a call to remember, as Rumi quoted, that we are all fragments of the same eternal source, seeking the very "ocean" we already belong to. It is both a cry against division and a reminder of the sacred truth that *we are one.*

Rise simply recalls the idea that separation is an illusion – created by the ego, by internal and external systems, and by fear. The soul's journey is to dissolve these illusions and remember the unity we share with each other, the earth, and the universe.

"Oneness" is not just philosophical – it is sacred. It is the essence of being, the truth beneath all chaos.

No matter who we are or where we stand, we share the same cosmic backdrop. The sun, sky, moon and stars are eternal witnesses to our shared humanity, symbols of interconnectedness that transcends time and space. They guide us to rise above the smallness of division, and to see the infinite beauty of our shared journey.

The drop of water, symbolizes the individual – unique, finite, yet inseparably part of the infinite ocean. This seems to be part of the human experience: we search for meaning, connection and purpose, not realizing that we already *are* the very thing we seek. The ocean is not something to find – it is something to remember. The journey is not outward, but inward.

Break the system – the corrupt internal systems that govern the mind, need to be taken down first before we demand to see change in external systems.

The "war against war" is not just a battle against external conflict, but against the inner wars we fight – wars of doubt and fear. To rise is to break free from these chains. Rise, emphasizes the idea that destruction is a necessary part of creation – by tearing down the veils to reveal the truth. This fight is to heal, to dismantle what divides us so that we can return to unity.

The war is not one of violence but of awakening. It is a collective call to action, urging humanity to rise above hatred, division and greed and to embrace love, unity and wholeness.

In Rise, this love is not passive. It is active, transformative and revolutionary, to end the wars within and without. Like drops of water, we may feel small and scattered, but together, we are the ocean – eternal, infinite, and inseparable.

IAM

Project I Am

I am

I am the one who walked in shadow

Hiding from my light

I am all my fears combined

Left behind, that I've left behind

Now I'm blazing like the sun

Shining every hour

10 to the 11th power

Once upon a time I thought I wasn't

Once upon a time I questioned, am I

Am I the one who leaves this legacy

Am I the one who sings this prophecy

Now I know the truth, now I speak my truth

Once upon a time

I am the King to my Queen

I am the Light to my Shadow

Dopamine, serotonin

I am the equilibrium to my pandemonium

Now I know my truth

I walk with God I walk with God

Now I speak my truth, I walk with God

PROJECT I AM:
The Lyrics

This is an execution (I walk with God, walk with God)

Code blue, code blue

Taking my last breath

Now I'm alive

I'm alive

Demons laying at my feet

I'm the one who sets me free

Free, I am free

Free, I am free

PROJECT I AM: *The Chapter*

Whether Buddhist, Muslim, Hindu, Christian or Jew, this song is for you, respectfully, and with love.

At the heart of *Project I Am* lies an awakening, inspired by Elizabeth Prophet's teachings on the Violet Flame, this song carries a vibrational key, keys we all have but may not know it.

In spiritual teachings, the I AM presence is regarded as the highest affirmation of "divine existence" within oneself.

"I am" acknowledges the self in its most raw and undefined state, aligning one with divine truth – in the full embodiment of their highest self.

Light, like in photophobia, is not always comforting. Sometimes it is blinding, something that must be hidden from, until one is strong enough to wield it.

Here, to "walk in shadow" is not to be lost, but to prepare.

Overcoming fear, we can render it meaningless – and transcend it completely.

To *blaze like the sun* is to become the fire you once were afraid would burn you. "Illuminated".

"10 to the 11th power" here is a mathematical expression, signifying limitless energy and infinite expansion.

Speaking one's truth is the final step – to no longer fear one's voice, one's light. While knowing is an internal realization, speaking is external embodiment. A way for our thoughts to turn into an active force in the world.

The pathway to balance lies in mastering the mind and emotion. Acquiring a spiritual and biological harmony is needed, so even where pandemonium exists, we are no longer ruled by it. Instead, we become the center of our own storm.

To *walk with God* is not about claiming dominion over others, nor is it about wielding power for personal glory. It is about alignment. It is an act of devotion, knowing we are connected to a source beyond. *I walk with God –* not as a conqueror but as a vessel.

The term *execution* is significant – as the final and irreversible end of the old self. While "code blue" signifies medical emergencies, here it is a signal of rebirth, as the last breath, in a plot twist of sorts, is when the true self emerges, fully alive.

Each line is a step in the journey to ultimate freedom. When truth is spoken, we set ourselves free, leaving a legacy. You do not need this book to tell you, that we are all already connected to God, Source and the Universe in ways unimaginable to the human mind. We are here together to remind each other of the truth we already know.

I am, just as you are.

Pain : Your Chapter

This is my chance to honor your journey, wherever you are on your chosen path, these pages are yours to create on and if you got this far, thank you dear Reader, you are indeed dear to me. Here is the instrumental version of "Pain", dedicated to you.

Suggestion: Light an unscented candle symbolizing the resilience within you. Close your eyes and let the shadows dance. Take slow, deep breaths. With each inhale, imagine drawing the essence of ancient wisdom of our ancestors embedded within you. With each exhale, release the weight of your suffering like smoke dissolving into the dark. This is an invitation with love, to rewrite your story, but only if you choose to.

PAIN: *YOUR CHAPTER*

To be Written

To be Written

Intertwined : Unfinished

This is an unfinished chapter, written as I break free from an unseen mental prison, walking through my darkness, for a redemption of the soul. I held myself captive in this Shawshank of the mind, with walls made of fear, guilt and self-doubt. It is a jailbreak through invisible tunnels until I reach the other side, of me, to find you. From feeling like the outsider who never belonged, finally coming home to versions of me, in you. I know you, are somewhere on the other side of this tunnel, and so this chapter remains unfinished. I do not know how this chapter ends, I am simply in a state of peace, in the knowing that we are, and always have been, intertwined.

Lyrics:

We're the misfits

We don't fit in

And I feel whole again

Home in my skin

We were never apart

Just a part of me

I couldn't see

Remembering me,

Is remembering you.

Unconfine

Undefine

The day I find me

Is the day I find you

Home.

We're home…Intertwined

Can you feel me?

Home…

Home again

We're home we're whole

We're whole again.

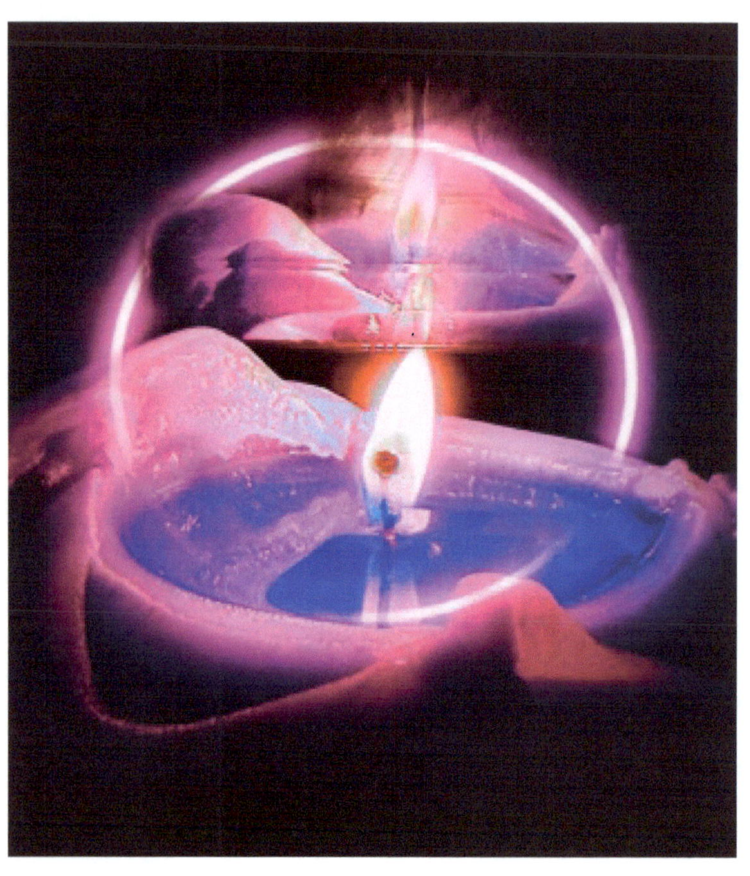

"We are all reflections of our eternal flame and infinite potential. Now, through the darkness, you are part of my journey just as much as I am a part of yours."

www.ingramcontent.com/pod-product-compliance
Lightning Source LLC
Chambersburg PA
CBHW040916110726

48005CB00006B/912